I0224663

You Can't Get There from Here

poems by

Margaret J. Vann

Finishing Line Press
Georgetown, Kentucky

You Can't Get There from Here

Copyright © 2021 by Margaret J. Vann
ISBN 978-1-64662-528-4 First Edition
All rights reserved under International and Pan-American Copyright Conventions.
No part of this book may be reproduced in any manner whatsoever without written
permission from the publisher, except in the case of brief quotations embodied in
critical articles and reviews.

ACKNOWLEDGMENTS

"Oneonta" appeared in 2008: *Poets' Choice*, and
2010: *Something More Solid Than Earth*

"Dragon Memories" appeared in 2012: *Poets' Choice*

"Black Mountain Reverie" appeared in 2013: *Poets' Choice*

"Susan Moore," "Advice from the Matriarch" appeared in 2014: *Poets' Choice*

"Remembrance" appeared in March 2014 *Where the Soul Sails*

"Back Roads" appeared in 2017: *Poets' Choice*

"Newsome Sinks" appeared in 2017: *The Red Cord*

"A Spill of Daffodils" appeared in 2020 *Poets' Choice*

Art work by Ann Vann, 2020

Publisher: Leah Huete de Maines
Editor: Christen Kincaid
Cover Art: Ann Vann
Author Photo: Life Touch
Cover Design: Elizabeth Maines McCleavy

Order online: www.finishinglinepress.com
also available on amazon.com

Author inquiries and mail orders:
Finishing Line Press
P. O. Box 1626
Georgetown, Kentucky 40324
U. S. A.

Table of Contents

Book 4—Places

Are We There Yet?

Plaintive words heard from the backseats of cars: are we there yet?

And every journey has to begin, and sometimes I can't get there from here. But...

These words:
a gift, a help piece, a friend's hand to ease the way into poetry
inspiration mixed with knowledge and bound in trial and try
perhaps even into essay
a place for words sewed with emotion and recollected passion
a place to ponder, to weight, to heft the sights and sounds of words at play

[Even now Sweet Baby Sister chews the eraser, needle teeth marking the edges of the book, her tail, my hand—I laugh in delight—new kitten.]

Book 1—Journeys

Thoughts While Listening to a Lecture on Discernment

"Jesus Christ, son of God, have mercy on me a sinner."

Let us have order—let us move from A to B to C—
let us know the road map
let us participate in the lesson

What is the lesson?
are there too many lessons?
are the holes in the net too large?
can the listener be captured?

Sometimes it is good to learn from the audience
this audience is polite
but far away—very far away—oh so far away
so what is the point?

Do we escape the message because there is no end
there is no particular lesson
because there is no order
no A to B to C—
nothing to discern

Driving

Driving
Alone with the radio and receding taillights ahead

Driving
Past rimed fields in the fog to somewhere new

Driving
Chatting with far-removed friends and the sky

Driving
Laughing with Bob and Red

Driving
Exclaiming over owl and hawk to my radio friends

Driving
Away from cares and into arms

Driving

Journey

Roads

On Sunday afternoons
we'd load the six or seven of us into the car
and drive through the countryside

I viewed those drives with mixed feeling.
I loved the scenery but got violently carsick
"Stop the car, Carl, Margaret needs to throw up."

Later in steamy Valdosta,
we would pile into our 2-door '39 Ford, Betsy
drive the hot summer nights
from Valdosta to Quitman and back

Daddy drove
it was a respite
we wanted the breeze—
lying on the shelf behind the backseat
I had a surcease from carsickness

I don't remember conversation—
only the moon slipping through the slash pines
and the sound of motor and tires
carrying me away

Ohio

When we traveled to visit Grandmother Lile
we would stop at state parks
where we peed, ran, ate our picnic lunch
and ran some more
before we crawled back into Betsy
to continue our way

An ancient mound
serpentined through the woods
and held an egg in its open mouth—
we would trace its length
and wonder

The burial mounds were tall
with stairs and rails to preserve
the mounds from eroding paths
Again—wonder

Don't really remember much of those long trips
from Valdosta to New Philadelphia
but I remember the mounds
and the wonder

Texas

From Huntsville, Alabama, to Pueblo, Colorado,
We went through Mississippi
got lost in Memphis, Tennessee,
then onto Arkansas, Oklahoma, the panhandle of Texas,
and a right turn into Colorado

In a woody '49 Ford station wagon
with three adults and four children from 14 to 8
no air conditioning—July
Hot—oh yes, it was hot
We'd stop buy ice
fill the fuchsia aluminum pitcher
and our aluminum tumblers with the chipped ice
keeping our cool

But it was in Texas or Oklahoma
where we picked up the hitchhiking priest—
well, he was dressed in black and wearing a collar
We were packed so full with the luggage and lunch supplies
that Daddy let down the tailgate
the priest rode out there until we got to Amarillo
So there we were: the eight of us looking like gypsies:
three adults, four children, and a priest on the tailgate

Life's Road Signs

We have so many signs along our way
As we move thru cuts and canyons
we are offered
rock falls and *falling rock.*

Do *rock falls* mean to watch the sky
or admire the wreck of passion by the road?
Falling rocks calls for caution—
looking about and wondering
if falling in love
happens to be as chancy
as *falling rocks* from above?

And when we fall in love
does the *earth move?*
Or does the *earth slide*
from beneath us leaving us
on *loose gravel* or *soft shoulders?*

No *standing* with ice on *bridges*—
no *standing* before the onslaught of love
that throws us a *sharp curve*
and leaves us with *water over the road*
water over our heads
drowning in love.

Remembrance

Whenever I drive by a winter woods
and look into the depths
carpeted with umber leaf litter
I remember

I remember the warm winter sun
on my face
the feel of crisp leaves beneath my back
the skeleton shadows of trees

I remember you
by my side
our hands touching
the smell of damp earth

I don't remember
what we talked bout
although we exchanged
smiles and laughter

I remember
we were just happy to be looking
through the empty branches
feeling the sun upon our faces

Winter woods, leaf litter
bring back memories
of sweet love/companionship
that has grown cold as winter woods.

II

Winter woods, leaf litter
bring back memories
of sweet love/companionship
that has grown cold as winter woods.

I remember
we were just happy to be looking
through the empty branches
feeling the sun upon our faces

I don't remember
what we talked about
although we exchanged
smiles and laughter

I remember you
by my side
our hands touching
the smell of damp earth

I remember the warm winter sun
on my face
the feel of crisp leaves beneath my back
the skeleton shadows of trees

I remember umber leaf litter
carpeted into the depths
and a winter woods
Whenever I drive by

2 Men with the Blues

She lay languid
the voice of Willie caressing her bare body
as Winton blew out her mind
She quivered in delight
and anticipation
while Willie washed over her

As the music drew to a close
She shivered—such pleasure

Modern Prometheus

patchwork man
assembled in pride
stolen

assembled: torso here attached to uneven legs, basic feet
        brawny arms, work-worn hands
        laid out in man shape
stitched: feather-stitch? chain stitch? running stitch? love knot?
        were all the man parts included?
        of course, a phallus, someone's family jewels…
        did the plumbing work?
wherefore came the heart?
        was it embroidered in place?
was there room for the padding of desire and a stomach for pain?

was the brain too ripe for rational thought?
        or having tasted death
was it ill-fitted for its revival?
        jaded? angry at being awakened?

O, patchwork man
quilted together with pride

Were you unbound & let go?
What fire did your assemblage bring to earth?

Memory

On the way to my last lover,
I traveled in early morn
leaving warm bed behind
to satisfy a rising heat within.
I found him sleep drenched
easily aroused—
a time of excitement and joy
too soon dispelled.

Too soon dispelled,
a time of excitement and joy
easily aroused.
I found him sleep drenched
to satisfy a rising heat within.
Leaving warm bed behind,
I traveled in early morn
on the way to my last lover.

Book 2—Exotic

Exotic fare

They keep coming those Cuban stamps:
José Martí, Ché, Fidel
All stare at me from envelopes
to quicken my mail carrier's heart
quicken my heart with memories

Sun-drenched ruins
brilliant colors faded to the same dull grey
narrow streets with shaded walkways
colonnades around central plazas
water plashing in tall fountains

I remember
smiles embraces kisses
hand holding & strolls through moonlit streets
carriage rides & languidly dancing the rumba
I remember

In these envelopes of tissue
come to my mailbox from so far away
so long ago—
the lover I found &
nuestros corazones—our hearts

China I: July 1982

I   Racing clouds obscure
     a waxing Chinese half-moon
     dragons devour moon.

II   Walls to exclude climb
     steep scarps, twist along narrow
     valleys, and decay.

III Ancient peoples smile
     and murmur "xie xie" as I
     snap their picture—shy.

China II: Bamboo Forest

Stone turtles, bearing
monoliths beneath roofless
temples, smile through time.

Etched by time and rain,
they hold exhortations for
all who read the stone.

Patiently, the son
of a dragon stands under
turning stars. He has

no lion to bar
his door to foreign scratches:
U.S.S. DEC '04.

Into the Woods

There   look over there
Do you see him
I looked into the winter woods
No

There   his hand on my arm
turning me   There
see he moved
I looked again
No

He took me by my shoulders
turning me   There see his rack
All I saw were limbs and brush and trees
No

I pulled loose and walked away
looking into the woods

I sit in the quiet dark
listening to my cicadas
waiting for the rain
and remember

In a Cool Season

I remember a year, a season
the two of them
sitting above the sea
looking down, down to the sea.

Alone

The two sat alone and felt
more than saw the season
withering the ferns in the old castle's walls—
withering the feelings they once shared.

So they waited amid a tumbled ruin
of dreams and love
watching the churning waves dash into foam.

The cold world was the
cliff and the surrounding season
of those two
who had drunk so deeply of love—
those two
who had now but the dregs of a once sweet wine.

Below the ruined castle,
flooding tides still break on the sand, and they—
they are still waiting
alone
with their warmth
in a cool season.

Beware

beware
spring
sweet lies false promise
3-leaved beauty & copper diamond coils
not bears not cougars not here
narrow roads & narrow paths
steep, steep drops
untethered boulders
silent deadfalls
algae-covered rocks
black-water eddies
algae-covered rocks
silent deadfalls
untethered boulders
steep, steep drops
narrow roads & narrow paths
not bears not cougars not here
3-leaved beauty & copper diamond coils
sweet lies false promise
spring
beware

Book 3—Home

.

Dragon Memories

In Dennison, an evening's entertainment
was going to the train station
to watch the big munitions trains
from Cleveland, Dayton, somewhere pass through.
Great fire-breathing locomotives
belching steam and sparks
whistling foreboding calls pulling flat cars
loaded with tanks, cannons, and trucks.
We'd wave and yell as they passed by.

Sometimes we'd see coaches
filled with young men   (no, boys)
grinning, hanging out of the windows
riding their rolling thunder to Valhalla.
The pretty girls waved their handkerchiefs and called
encouragement to the young warriors
on their way to exotic places.

Thrilled by the spectacle of hissing, flaming trains
roaring thru the station,
but too young to understand
what I was seeing.
Too young, to understand it was
Death riding those rails behind iron dragons.

Homecoming

I don't remember when
Daddy came home from the war

I remember his being away
the letters he wrote Mama
the strange place in north Georgia
Smyrna so far away
[but now so close to New Philly]

Daddy sent oranges and tangerines
that we were allotted one section at a time
He sent semi-sweet Hersey chocolate bars
that we were allotted one square at a time
How I savored that dark chocolate that melted on my tongue
[I still eat my dark chocolate savoring each small bite]

I remember the empty place in their bed
the empty place in my heart—my world
[Mama said I didn't smile
the whole time he was gone.]
But his homecoming was so wonderful
I can't remember it at all—
not at all

May Queen

Eight of us after a long drive in early February
from Ohio to Valdosta
untangled limbs & pulled sleepy-eyed
into warm, dark room
white-haired man rocking by the fire—
not "hello"—not "welcome"
but: "Give me the baby" the baby—Sarah
I stared in wonder as Sarah gurgled
while this new grandfather sang:
"My gal's a corker; she's a New Yorker."

Off to first grade in a brick castle
learning new books
Jerry & friends were the stars—not Dick & Jane
more to read—dear Jack fell down the hill
and broke his head not a gold crown
Who were my new friends at Central Grammar?
We played Red Rover, tag.

I grew snaggle-toothed;
Mama cut uneven bangs as I squirmed
But I was crowned May Queen for the pageant.
Dressed in green-dyed gauze tunic
with flower-tipped bamboo scepter
surrounded by my elvan court, I smile.

All summer I reigned as Queen on Central Avenue
with Edna Viola as my princess attendant
with not so worshipful brothers as guards
The summer lasted only—forever

So I am May Queen only—forever.

Advice from the Matriarch

"Don't sit on the edge of the seat, you may fly off and be killed.
I know a mother whose child sat on the edge of the seat;
and when the dad had to stop suddenly,
why that child flew off the seat into the windshield
and its brains dropped down into its mother's lap."
This is some of the first advice I remember Mama offering.

"Crack your eggs into a small bowl
before you add them to the batter.
Why I remember someone who cracked an egg
into her cake batter and out came a dead baby chick.
Had to throw the whole mess away."
Mama's specialties were pies and grilled cheese;
in the summer we fixed our own potted meat sandwiches.
But she did cook a mean biscuit using bacon grease for the lard.

"Never pass up an opportunity to use a bathroom."
On long trips [and ours always seemed to be,
for we would be going to Ohio to visit Grandmother Lile
or back home to Valdosta],
Mama nor Daddy, when he came along,
was into many bathroom stops.
We'd stop for gas and picnic lunches
but nowhere in between;
so if you hadn't gone when you had the chance,
 you had a long wait.

"When going around a curve,
don't take it on the inside.
Why I know a Mother who always
took her curves on the inside;
and when her daughter learned to drive,
she did like her mama. Got killed
by an oncoming car on the inside of the curve."
I believed her 'cause my Mama drove a stick shift,
two-door '39 Ford nonstop
all the way up Highway 41
from Valdosta, Georgia, to
New Philadelphia, Ohio, with six children.
She had to know the safe way.

Spaces

Look at this picture.
It was taken at their 50th anniversary.
Everyone is there,
but that space for the one in jail.

Oops, as I look new spaces appear:
        She has gone to meet her late husband.
        He just faded away.
Over there by Aunt Louise,
        he is shrinking into himself.

New spaces appear as one-by-one
        the old ones drift off
in mind and memory
        the young change spaces
fill more space
become suddenly the old ones.

Look into her eyes,
        see the reflection
of her mother, maybe her father?

Just look at this picture.
How have all the places become
        empty space?

Unaware

Boulder

Unprepared to see what I caught—
a look unaware and there dressed
to attend, in my clothes I thought,
her grandson's wedding was my blesséd
late mother. Why hadn't I seen
her before? Was she a dream?

A look unaware, unprepared
to see my mama, in my clothes,
at her grandson's wedding—joy shared
she, a dream, even to her toes
painted just like mine. Was that me
holding the wine or did I see—

How did she get those clothes? Mother
dressed in my jacket and beads. Too
late, not aware I was looking
at a picture of me/Mother?

Empty

Each has within
a place

Measured by what is not there
a place we hide
even from ourselves
Trying for a time
to keep yesterday
from swallowing
tomorrow.

Such is a shallow life
ignoring place and people—
life bound
about with spaces and secrets
Concealed in idle words
empty talk
careless love.

Book 4—Places

Oneonta

Oneonta, on the Florida short route, had nothing to slow
the Yankees headed to the beach except—
2 right-angle turns
no Dairy Queen, no MacDonald's, no drive in/dine in

A red Christmas star marks the spot where
once puce-blossomed kudzu blanketed
the hillside and building
falling into a rectangular hole

In those days before air conditioning
young people spent their summers days at the pool
Boys strutted their tanned, hard bodies
Girls, basted in baby oil and iodine, lay on towels
cutting their eyes at the bronzed lifeguards

The boys jack-knifed or cannonballed
into the pool splashing the girls on the towels
The bright girls never swam—
sometimes sitting with their feet in the water
and splashing themselves to cool off
in the hot Alabama sun

In the 50s the pool—the pool of summer days
for tanned white girls & boys
would now have to let
black girls & black boys
swim in that self-same pool
The wise men of Oneonta knew how
to protect their little dark white girls
from sharing the pool water with black boys
[never mind no black families
lived in Blount County]

The wise men closed the pool
drained the pool, boarded up the pool house,
chained the gate, and
turned their backs

Kudzu ran down the hillside,
up over the fence, and into the pool
covered the area in green & puce
covered the laughter, splashing, strutting
The star—remember the star?
At Christmastime it shone over the pool—

Now the star lit the kudzu with its puce blossoms.
The kudzu grew & grew
crept over and into the pool house, filled the pool
New life, maybe dangerous, moved into the kudzu jungle.

Again the wise men acted
cleaned up the kudzu, razed the pool house,
filled the pool, smoothed the area,
and left the Star
to brood over an empty parking lot

Susan Moore

My hamlet

"Women are nothing; wives and mothers are everything."
That's what my Daddy said.
I believed him, for I was the quiet, good girl.
I wasn't the beautiful nor the smart daughter.
No schooling for me as I was to be a wife and mother.
So at 15 I married the richest man in the village—
Dutifully I had his babies and kept his house.
Quietly I saved to pay a tutor to further my schooling.
My husband indulged me.
But at 21 I ran off with the tutor and my boys
who were reared to value women for themselves—
to value education for all.

Now I, Susan Moore, lie on this grassy hillside
overlooking the school my sons built to honor my wish
that our village have a school for boys and girls—
the village now named for me.
Daddy died before seeing the difference that women make,
for out of nothing came a school and a village.

after the style of Edgar Lee Masters'
Spoon River Anthology

Black Mountain Reverie

In Black Mountain Hollow,
above Lakey Gap Creek on the Blue Ridge path,
I found, first, faded Trillium *grandiflora,*
then, lady slipper orchids gone to seed,
and in those hemlock woods,
sheltered by a gnarled, scaly apple tree,
a run-away forsythia grove
surrounded the remains
of an ancient hearth & chimney.
Nothing was left of the old home site
but the forsythia, apple tree, hearth & chimney.

I wondered at the woman
who climbed down to the creek
and back up to her one-room home.
Did she plant the forsythia as a cutting
taken from her mother's yard?
Did the apple tree shade a stoop of sandstone
where the children played? There had to be children.

Did she find pleasure in the mountain laurel
and piedmont azaleas along her path to the creek?
I hope she had a touch of beauty in the cabin too—
a blue willow plate, a piece of cobalt glass.
Was she lonesome?
Was her man gone all day to work the bottom land?

Did she fear the dark woods around her?
Woods she set afire with the blooming forsythia.
What sets fire to isolated lives
as the forsythia set fire to her spring woods?
She of the ruined fireplace above Lakey Gap Creek,
was her life better?

Song

For Cades Cove

Cicadas sing in my ear
reminding me of another time
another place

Another place set in a bowl
of meadows, woods, and
streams surrounded
by haze-covered mountains

Another time held in place
empty cabins weed-filled gardens
bereft of the people
who loved, built, and lived there

Cicadas that those early folks
heard as part of summer's rhythm
Cicadas that sing visitors to sleep
in campground and tent
beneath second-growth forest

Cicadas that remind me
of a time when I was crazy
in love with woods and man and flowers
the roar of cicadas

I sit in the quiet dark
listening to my cicadas
waiting for the rain
and remember

Heartland

The soul is faithless but will return to the LORD
Jaydeva paraphrase

Hope moves into
Empty spaces made void
After the upheaval of earthquake, fire, flood
Regret
Tell me a love story …
Love story of lovers with Hope
Ancient love stories where
None die   none face
Death in Heartland

Newsome Sinks

            I
The sky grows greener
outside my window
as spring eases in
            II
under sketchy, green-pink netting
wood hyacinths grow: light lavender haze
crawling up sinks

across the fern-gladéd floor
a hillside dressed
in green & white

trillium nodding
in a spring breeze
subtle scents mingle
            III
if I close my eyes
even now—
I catch a whiff of early spring
and am transported
again

Heart Place

lying in the spring dark
listening to the water rush to meet the sea
looking beyond the tree tops
catching the new moon cradling her sister

one by one stars emerge
Orion has already fled the sky
to return another season
as Venus tries to catch Diana

here in my heart place
I hear the whip-poor-will chant
and the owl questioning
my presence without you.

"... into the wilderness for nourishment for a time, and times, and half a time."

We search for our nourishment—
some in the city—some in books—
but I and mine
we search
in the wilderness among the boulders
beneath the trees & beside the running waters
in the cool of a season
we search always
around the next bend or over the next rise or
in the quiet shade
for a time
and times
and half a time
and sometimes just
sometimes
we find our nourishment
for a time
and times
and half a time
sometimes

Summer Fire

I say:

Go out!　　　　Go out!
Enjoy the show!

Summer is the time

of orange and yellow roadsides—
coneflower and butterfly weed
that glow in floral flame

There!　　　　on shaded limestone ledges
native hydrangea drapes
its white lacy blossoms

Wood's edge restrains white panicles
of oak leaf hydrangea—
blossoms blushing as they age

Butterflies flutter about
tall summer phlox that echoes
blush of hydrangea

Go out!　　　　Go out!
Hit the road again.
Enjoy the show!

Back Roads

Back roads have taken me
through forests, hamlets,
by lonesome cemeteries
along rivers and rusted railroads

These back roads are a comfort to me
to be again among pine woods,
in red clay hills, and by black-water swamps—
places of my childhood

I was on my way home from visiting
my mother in Valdosta.
She was on her way home too—
home to be with her belovèd Carl

Daddy couldn't find bridges
Would there be bridges to cross
Mama was the navigator on their road trips
she would be able to cross this last bridge

I traveled each weekend
to be with Mama as she slipped away
Every trip was one last time to see her
until it was the last time

I traveled down a narrow 2-lane road
in a driving rain on a road without power lines
to mark the presence of fellow beings
with John Denver singing
"Country Roads" as the rain fell

traveling still on the back roads of memory
I enrich my time here now
I travel the slow back roads
to the future
savoring every mile
looking for each landmark
with a smile
it is here I belong

Margaret Jones Vann, a longtime resident of Huntsville, Alabama, has been writing since her graduate poetry class with the late Dr. Augustus Mason at UA in Tuscaloosa. Her poems have been published in small magazines, including *Muse, The Scribbler, Red Mountain Rendezvous, Poem,* and *The Sampler.* This is her second book of poetry as she has a chapbook, *Can This Be Heaven?* also published by Finishing Line Press. Margaret's voice can be heard on WLRH reading for the Sun Dial Writers. One of her favorite pastimes is road trips. Give her gas money and a destination, and she is gone. Road trips have offered her many subjects for poems. Margaret has a wild(flower) garden, two rescue cats, five extraordinary grandchildren, and now a fine great-grandson.

www.ingramcontent.com/pod-product-compliance
Lightning Source LLC
Chambersburg PA
CBHW031220090426
42740CB00009B/1244